MW00489883

FROM THE LIBRARY OF:

_ _ _ _ _ _ _ _ _ _ _ _ _ _ _

_ _ _ _ _ _ _ _ _ _ _ _ _ _ _

_ _ _ _ _ _ _ _ _ _ _ _ _ _ _

YOU CAN NEVER get a cup of tea LARGE ENOUGH OR a book long enough TO SUIT ME.

C.S. Lewis

very firm, and
quaintance's
ch. At the sa
e loved to pa
ely made up o
honists; rather
us quality, like

BOOKS ARE THE PLANE,
and the train, and the road.
THEY ARE THE DESTINATION,
and the journey. They are home.

ANNA QUINDLEN

EVERYTHING *in the* WORLD EXISTS IN ORDER *to end up* *as a* BOOK.

STÉPHANE MALLARMÉ

THE BEST MOMENTS IN READING

are when you come across something—

A THOUGHT, A FEELING,

a way of looking at things—which

YOU HAD THOUGHT SPECIAL

and particular to you.

AND NOW, HERE IT IS,

set down by someone else,

A PERSON YOU HAVE NEVER MET,

someone even who is long dead.

AND IT IS AS IF A HAND HAS

come out, and taken yours.

ALAN BENNETT

●●●●●

BOOKS ARE
a uniquely portable magic.

STEPHEN KING

●●●●●●

FOR SOME OF US,

books are as important as

ALMOST ANYTHING ELSE ON EARTH.

What a miracle it is that

OUT OF THESE SMALL, FLAT, RIGID

squares of paper unfolds

WORLD AFTER WORLD AFTER WORLD,

worlds that sing to you,

COMFORT AND QUIET OR EXCITE YOU.

Anne Lamott

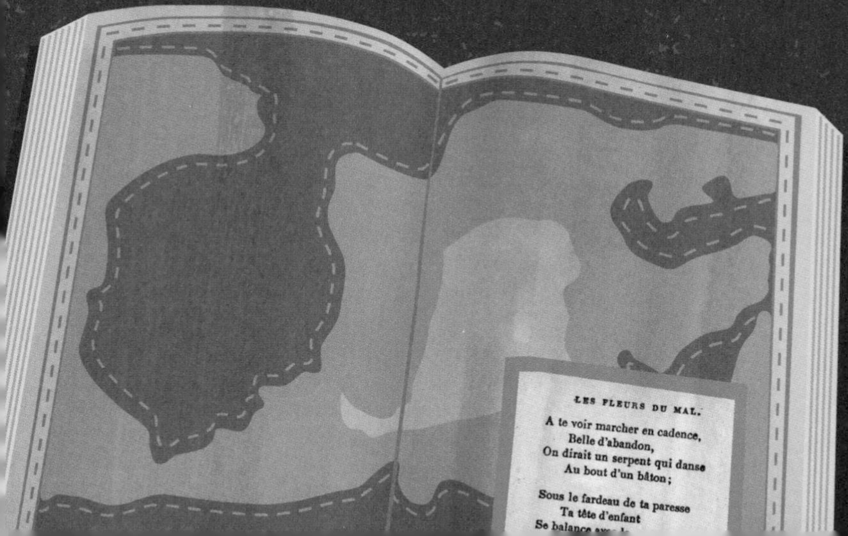

LES FLEURS DU MAL.

A te voir marcher en cadence,
Belle d'abandon,
On dirait un serpent qui danse
Au bout d'un bâton;

Sous le fardeau de ta paresse
Ta tête d'enfant
Se balance

WE READ BOOKS TO
find out who we are.
WHAT OTHER PEOPLE,
real or imaginary,
DO AND THINK AND FEEL
...is an essential guide
TO OUR UNDERSTANDING
of what we ourselves are
AND MAY BECOME.

Ursula K. LeGuin